From Neurons to Neighborhoods

An Update

WORKSHOP SUMMARY

Committee on *From Neurons to Neighborhoods*: Anniversary Workshop

Board on Children, Youth, and Families

Steve Olson, *Rapporteur*

INSTITUTE OF MEDICINE *AND*
NATIONAL RESEARCH COUNCIL
OF THE NATIONAL ACADEMIES

THE NATIONAL ACADEMIES PRESS
Washington, D.C.
www.nap.edu

THE NATIONAL ACADEMIES PRESS • 500 Fifth Street, NW • Washington, DC 20001

NOTICE: The project that is the subject of this report was approved by the Governing Board of the National Research Council, whose members are drawn from the councils of the National Academy of Sciences, the National Academy of Engineering, and the Institute of Medicine. The members of the committee responsible for the report were chosen for their special competences and with regard for appropriate balance.

This project was supported by IOM Healthy Kids Communication Campaign. Any opinions, findings, conclusions, or recommendations expressed in this publication are those of the author(s) and do not necessarily reflect the view of the organizations or agencies that provided support for this project.

International Standard Book Number-13: 978-0-309-20978-6
International Standard Book Number-10: 0-309-20978-1

Additional copies of this report are available from the National Academies Press, 500 Fifth Street, NW, Keck 360, Washington, DC 20001; (800) 624-6242 or (202) 334-3313, http://www.nap.edu.

For more information about the Institute of Medicine, visit the IOM home page at: **www.iom.edu.**

Suggested citation: IOM (Institute of Medicine) and NRC (National Research Council). 2012. *From Neurons to Neighborhoods: An Update: Workshop Summary.* Washington, DC: The National Academies Press.

THE NATIONAL ACADEMIES
Advisers to the Nation on Science, Engineering, and Medicine

The **National Academy of Sciences** is a private, nonprofit, self-perpetuating society of distinguished scholars engaged in scientific and engineering research, dedicated to the furtherance of science and technology and to their use for the general welfare. Upon the authority of the charter granted to it by the Congress in 1863, the Academy has a mandate that requires it to advise the federal government on scientific and technical matters. Dr. Ralph J. Cicerone is president of the National Academy of Sciences.

The **National Academy of Engineering** was established in 1964, under the charter of the National Academy of Sciences, as a parallel organization of outstanding engineers. It is autonomous in its administration and in the selection of its members, sharing with the National Academy of Sciences the responsibility for advising the federal government. The National Academy of Engineering also sponsors engineering programs aimed at meeting national needs, encourages education and research, and recognizes the superior achievements of engineers. Dr. Charles M. Vest is president of the National Academy of Engineering.

The **Institute of Medicine** was established in 1970 by the National Academy of Sciences to secure the services of eminent members of appropriate professions in the examination of policy matters pertaining to the health of the public. The Institute acts under the responsibility given to the National Academy of Sciences by its congressional charter to be an adviser to the federal government and, upon its own initiative, to identify issues of medical care, research, and education. Dr. Harvey V. Fineberg is president of the Institute of Medicine.

The **National Research Council** was organized by the National Academy of Sciences in 1916 to associate the broad community of science and technology with the Academy's purposes of furthering knowledge and advising the federal government. Functioning in accordance with general policies determined by the Academy, the Council has become the principal operating agency of both the National Academy of Sciences and the National Academy of Engineering in providing services to the government, the public, and the scientific and engineering communities. The Council is administered jointly by both Academies and the Institute of Medicine. Dr. Ralph J. Cicerone and Dr. Charles M. Vest are chair and vice chair, respectively, of the National Research Council.

www.national-academies.org

v

Reviewers

This report has been reviewed in draft form by individuals chosen for their diverse perspectives and technical expertise, in accordance with procedures approved by the National Research Council's Report Review Committee. The purpose of this independent review is to provide candid and critical comments that will assist the institution in making its published report as sound as possible and to ensure that the report meets institutional standards for objectivity, evidence, and responsiveness to the study charge. The review comments and draft manuscript remain confidential to protect the integrity of the process. We wish to thank the following individuals for their review of this report:

Duane Alexander, National Institutes of Health
O. Marion Burton, University of South Carolina
P. Lindsay Chase-Landsale, Northwestern University
Sarah L. Friedman, CNA Corp.
Lonnie R. Sherrod, Society for Research in Child Development
Ross A. Thompson, University of California, Davis

Although the reviewers listed above have provided many constructive comments and suggestions, they were not asked to endorse the conclusions or recommendations nor did they see the final draft of the report before its release. The review of this report was overseen by **Jeanne Brooks-Gunn,** Columbia University. Appointed by the National Research Council and

Institute of Medicine, she was responsible for making certain that an independent examination of this report was carried out in accordance with institutional procedures and that all review comments were carefully considered. Responsibility for the final content of this report rests entirely with the authoring committee and the institution.

Contents

Preface

The original study *From Neurons to Neighborhoods: The Science of Early Childhood Development* was released at a press conference in the Washington, DC, headquarters of the National Academy of Sciences on October 3, 2000 (see Appendix A for the original committee membership and statement of task). For weeks before the event, study director Deborah Phillips and I, along with members of the Committee on Integrating the Science of Early Childhood Development, had been preparing diligently and hoping that our report would garner significant media coverage and have a major impact on policy makers. However, when the report was finally released, the findings of a 6-year investigation into President Bill Clinton's involvement in the Whitewater case were delivered to the Congress—and our carefully constructed announcement fell off the public's radar screen.

I'll never forget the words of Vanee Vines, the National Academies' press officer, who worked with us on the report and put our disappointment into a broader perspective. "This report is not a breaking news story," she said. "You have to give people time to read it carefully and digest its content. I promise you that this report will have legs."

More than a decade later, those words have held up well. *From Neurons to Neighborhoods*, the product of a 2.5-year study, has indeed had legs. Moreover—to extend the metaphor—it stood up and ran on those legs. It called for a fundamental reexamination of the nation's response to the needs of young children and families, drawing upon a wealth of scientific knowledge that had emerged in recent decades. The study shaped policy agendas and intervention efforts at national, state, and local levels. It captured a gratifying level of attention in the United States and around the world and has helped to foster a highly dynamic and increasingly visible science of early childhood development. It contributed to a growing public understanding of the foundational importance of the early childhood years and has stimulated a global conversation about the unmet needs of millions of young children.

Ten years later, on October 27-28, 2010, the Board on Children, Youth, and Families of the Institute of Medicine (IOM) and National Research Council (NRC), which shepherded the creation of *From Neurons to Neighborhoods*, held a 2-day workshop in Washington, DC, to review and commemorate a decade of advances related to the mission of the report. The workshop began with a series of highly interactive breakout sessions in which experts in early childhood development examined the four organizing themes of the original report and identified both measurable progress and remaining challenges; a summary of the themes and the conclusions of the breakout sessions appear in Chapter 1. A celebratory dinner on the evening of the first day brought together many of the people involved in the original funding, writing, and dissemination of the report to reflect on the reasons for its influence and to discuss future directions for the science of early childhood development and its application. The next day, six speakers chosen for their diverse perspectives on early childhood research and policy issues discussed how to build on the accomplishments of the past decade and to launch the next era in early childhood science, policy, and practice. Their perspectives, which are summarized in Chapters 2 and 3, are just illustrative of the many that could have been discussed at the workshop. Their talks provided a lively cross-section of reflections on the importance of the report and on future research and policy directions. My closing remarks at the workshop are summarized in the final chapter of this report.

From its inception, *From Neurons to Neighborhoods* has been driven by the proposition that there is a single, integrated science of early childhood development despite the extent to which it is carved up and divided among a diversity of professional disciplines, policy sectors, and service delivery systems. While much work still remains to be done toward this goal, one of the report's chief contributions was to identify that common base of knowledge on which researchers, educators, health care providers, courts, policy makers, civic leaders, and many other constituencies have been able to build. The presentations at the 2010 workshop demonstrate both the promise of this integrated science and the rich diversity of contributions to that science.

Perhaps the most rewarding source of gratification for the authoring committee is the extent to which *From Neurons to Neighborhoods* has helped transform the public discourse about young children. As stated on the last page of the report, our aim was to "mobilize the best available knowledge (and promote its continued growth) in order to move beyond simple questions about whether environments and early experiences make a difference." These concluding thoughts ended with a challenge "to answer questions about how to enhance the quality of those environments and experiences in an effort to promote the health and development of young children." As we take stock of what has been accomplished since those words were written, it is clear that significant progress has been made in answering the "why" question, while much remains to be done to answer questions that begin with "what, how, and what's next?" In this context, many of the toughest challenges today are variations on themes that were identified by the committee and articulated in the report more than a decade ago.

As the date for this anniversary celebration approached, I reread the acknowledgments section of the report and counted 123 people who contributed to its creation—far too many to thank individually again by name. That said, several key people deserve special mention beyond the 17 extraordinary members of the original study committee. Deborah Phillips was an inspiring and indefatigable study director who guided the report from its earliest conception through its writing, publication, and release. Much of the report's success should be credited to her extraordinary efforts. The 13 members of the IOM-NRC review committee provided us with a formidable stack of comments and suggestions that greatly improved the report, and our editors—Eugenia Grohman and Christine McShane—scrutinized every word of the manuscript before it was sent to the printer.

The anniversary event, *From Neurons to Neighborhoods*: Ten Years Later, was organized by Rosemary Chalk, the director of the Board on Children, Youth, and Families. Pamella Atayi, Reine Homawoo, Wendy Keenan, and Rachel Pittluck provided valuable assistance in organizing and running the event. Steve Olson wrote the summary, working from a transcript generated by Caset Associates, Ltd.

One of the most valuable pieces of advice that the Committee on Integrating the Science of Early Childhood Development received very early in the writing of *From Neurons to Neighborhoods* was that it should try to help build the knowledge base that would be needed 10 years in the future, not just address the pressing issues of the day. The content and energy displayed at the anniversary gathering for *From Neurons to Neighborhoods* indicate that the committee successfully embraced this advice. The past decade has seen immense progress, and the prospect of future advances in the domains of science, policy, and practice is even more exciting. The reassuring message that followed our less than auspicious release was prophetic. The science of early childhood development does indeed have legs!

Jack P. Shonkoff, *Chair*
Committee on *From Neurons to Neighborhoods*: Anniversary Workshop

1

From Neurons to Neighborhoods: Reflections on Four Themes

In *From Neurons to Neighborhoods: The Science of Early Childhood Development* (NRC and IOM, 2000), the Committee on Integrating the Science of Early Childhood Development organized its main conclusions and recommendations around four overarching themes:

1. All children are born wired for feelings and ready to learn.
2. Early environments matter and nurturing relationships are essential.
3. Society is changing and the needs of young children are not being addressed.
4. Interactions among early childhood science, policy, and practice are problematic and demand dramatic rethinking.

More than 10 years later, these themes still deserve attention. The workshop held to commemorate the anniversary of the report's release in 2011 consisted of two parts. On the first afternoon, 40 invited participants divided into four working groups to discuss the four broad themes. Their goals were to reflect on the continued relevance of the themes, discuss progress in the 10 years since the theme was identified, and point to future research and policy actions that could further realize the intent of each theme. Summaries of the working groups' main observations and conclusions, which are included below, were given by the rapporteurs at a plenary session following these discussions. Each summary is preceded by a relevant quotation from the 2000 report, *From Neurons to Neighborhoods*.

The second day of the workshop was a public session, which was also a video webcast to audiences throughout the United States as well as other countries. The program consisted of six invited presentations, which are summarized in Chapters 2 and 3 of this report. The archive of the video webcast (which includes the slides presented by each speaker) can be found at: http://www.iom.edu/Activities/Children/Neuronstoneighborhoods/2010-OCT-28.aspx.

The anniversary workshop and this publication were sponsored by the Healthy Kids Communication Campaign, supported by private gifts to the Institute of Medicine. Many of the workshop participants included individuals who had been involved with the original study *From Neurons to Neighborhoods*. Additional participants included representatives from government agencies, foundations, professional organizations, advocacy groups, and other researchers. The workshop thus offered an opportunity to share reflections from the original study with insights drawn from knowledge and experience that have emerged in the decade since its publication. Although the workshop was a celebratory activity, it is intended to stimulate future initiatives to synthesize and integrate the broad array of findings emerging from the many disciplines associated with the science of child development.

The workshop was organized and hosted by the Institute of Medicine (IOM) and the National Research Council (NRC) through the Committee on *From Neurons to Neighborhoods*: Anniversary Workshop within the IOM-NRC Board on Children, Youth, and Families. The board brings the multidisciplinary knowledge and analytic tools of the behavioral, health, and social sciences to bear on the development of policies, programs, and services for children, youth, and families. It informs deliberations about some of the critical issues facing communities, states, and the nation, including child health and health services, family support, child care, and early child development; biological and behavioral changes among children and youth; preschool education, school engagement, and youth development; child abuse, family violence, and child welfare; and the prevention of underage drinking and other risky and dangerous behaviors.

It is important to be specific about the nature of this report, which documents the information presented in the workshop presentations and discussions. Its purpose is to lay out the key ideas that emerged from the workshop, and this summary should be viewed as an initial step in building on new insights that have emerged since the publication of the original report. The report is confined to the material presented by the workshop speakers and participants. Neither the workshop nor this summary is intended as a comprehensive review of what is known about the topic, although it is a general reflection of the field. The presentations and discussions were limited by the time available for the workshop. A more comprehensive review and synthesis of relevant research knowledge will have to await future development.

This report was prepared by a rapporteur and does not represent findings or recommendations that can be attributed to the planning committee. Indeed, the report summarizes views expressed by workshop participants, and the committee is responsible only for its overall quality and accuracy as a record of what transpired at the workshop. Also, the workshop was not designed to generate consensus conclusions or recommendations but focused instead on the identification of ideas, themes, and considerations that contribute to the understanding of the topic.

Theme 1: All children are born wired for feelings and ready to learn.

From the time of conception to the first day of kindergarten, development proceeds at a pace exceeding that of any subsequent stage of life. Efforts to understand this process have revealed the myriad and remarkable accomplishments of the early childhood period, as well as the serious problems that confront some young children and their families long before school entry. A fundamental paradox exists and is unavoidable: development in the early years is both highly robust and highly vulnerable. Although there have been long-standing debates about how much the early years really matter in the larger scheme of lifelong development, our conclusion is unequivocal: What happens during the first months and years of life matters a lot, not because this period of development provides an indelible blueprint for adult well-being, but because it sets either a sturdy or fragile stage for what follows. (NRC and IOM, 2000, p. 4)

The observation that babies come into the world with emotions and the ability to learn raises the question of whether early childhood development actually starts at birth. In addition, an emphasis on the period immediately after birth can be detrimental if it is assumed that this period is a strict determinant of later development. Although the first few years of life can be critical for initiating trajectories, they do not determine them. Development is a continuum from the prenatal to the postnatal periods, with a particular influence from maternal nutrition, stress, and health. In that sense, starting with "birth" can be both too late and too early.

The word "wired" also can be problematic if incorrectly interpreted. That term can connote too much permanence, as if the brain were hard wired. But there is a diversity of wiring in the brain. Furthermore, this wiring constantly changes in response to biological and environmental influences. Again, trajectories provide a better way of thinking about development. The farther out in time, the greater the divergence among individuals. These differences can be reduced, although there are limits to plasticity.

The differences between individuals are not all positive or all negative. A difference can lead to advantages in one context and disadvantages in another. Differences sometimes are interpreted in terms of "atypicality"—

defining some people as normal and others as not normal. But there are more useful ways of thinking about differences. For example, differences can be systematic, leading to phenotypic clusters that are not well understood. Differences also can be interpreted in terms of responsivity: How much do people change in response to context?

The wiring of the brain has become an important consideration in research based on neuroimaging. The capability to visualize the structure and function of the brain is exciting but also raises issues. Neuroimaging lacks a developmental dimension, partly because the tools and protocols are not available to do imaging with young children. Also, the public and some quarters of the scientific community have gained the mistaken impression that neuroimaging can reveal a direct link between brain activation and sophisticated behaviors, even though such a link is extremely complex.

Another pressing issue is the integration of social-emotional development and cognitive development. Although the processes are integrated, they generally are not studied in an integrated way, nor are researchers trained to study them in an integrated way. Yet when the integration fails in individuals, serious problems can arise. An example is moral development. How can science study the development of values in young children? How are those values related to executive functions? And what are the roles of family and schools in forming values?

Finally, the wiring of the brain is related to the roles of biological and environmental factors in the developing child. The understanding of the genome has undergone a revolution in recent years, but there is no corresponding theoretical, methodological, or taxonomic understanding of critical environmental influences or concepts. Responsivity or sensitivity may offer a handle on some of these concepts, but an environmental framework for understanding development has yet to be created.

All of these issues have implications for the training of researchers, practitioners, policy makers, and the public. All these groups need to have some understanding of systems science, which encompasses the content of several disciplines. Yet researchers need to be an expert in some area while also being able to communicate with people in different disciplines.

Theme 2: Early environments matter and nurturing relationships are essential.

The scientific evidence on the significant developmental impacts of early experiences, caregiving relationships, and environmental threats is incontrovertible. Virtually every aspect of early human development, from the brain's evolving circuitry to the child's capacity for empathy, is affected by the environments and experiences that are encountered in a cumulative fashion, beginning early in the prenatal period and extending through-

out the early childhood years. The science of early development is also clear about the specific importance of parenting and of regular caregiving relationships more generally. The question today is not whether early experience matters, but rather how early experiences shape individual development and contribute to children's continued movement along positive pathways. (NRC and IOM, 2000, p. 6)

From Neurons to Neighborhoods placed great emphasis on social-emotional development, but public policies still slight this area. Part of the problem is the lack of valid assessments of development. Today the emphasis is on what is already being done and what can be measured. Researchers also know much more about the development of cognitive domains than they do about social-emotional development.

Educational assessments are a prominent issue in measuring the outcomes of learning. Today, policy makers have expectations of learning programs that are not grounded in research. Assessment strategies need to encourage teachers to teach with understanding. Yet current research is not compelling enough to move toward greatly improved assessments of learning. The challenge of developing better assessments is even greater with English language learners.

From Neurons to Neighborhoods was one of several reports that catalyzed conversations related to quality and access in education, which is also related to issues surrounding assessments. Having effective measurements and tools would help move early childhood education toward both greater quality and greater access. These measurements and tools also would contribute to the performance assessment of teachers, and they could provide a way to harness new knowledge and new technologies in early childhood education.

A prominent feature of conversations regarding quality and access has been the need to integrate science into early childhood initiatives, including training and professional development. Research conducted on curricula has been necessary but not sufficient. The larger question is how to bring science to bear on matters of practice to improve quality in classrooms and homes. This task also requires effective messaging for parents, teachers, and policy makers, so that science is translated into actions that are concrete and doable.

Have public policies and programs moved as far as they need to? The answer is clearly no. Large numbers of children are not served by early childhood education. Continued study of the benefits of early childhood development can continue to make the case for change. For example, policy makers should not think of early childhood education as a zero-sum game. Society will be better off by increasing quality and the number of children served.

Even 10 years after the publication of *From Neurons to Neighborhoods*, important questions remain: How can science be used to bring parents, policy makers, and other players together in a coordinated way? What are reasonable outcomes for children 5 years, 10 years, or 30 years after a program ends? Has human capital been overemphasized compared with children's well-being? *From Neurons to Neighborhoods* helped broaden the context of early childhood development, but this context still needs to be better integrated for scientific research to have maximum impact.

Theme 3: Society is changing and the needs of young children are not being addressed.

Profound social and economic transformations are posing serious challenges to the efforts of parents and others to strike a healthy balance between spending time with their children, securing their economic needs, and protecting them from the many risks beyond the home that may have an adverse impact on their health and development. (NRC and IOM, 2000, p. 8)

Are children better off today than they were 10 years ago? The general answer is that children are not as far along as people interested in early childhood development would like them to be. There have been pivotal changes, however. The idea that early childhood development is important has reached the consciousness of parents and policy makers. But the translation of scientific information into policy and systems change has not gone as far it needs to go. In addition, large disparities among population groups continue to exist and are growing.

It is more difficult to identify effective interventions for children ages 0 to 3 than for older age groups. One reason is that there is not the same infrastructure of programs and policies for young children. Again, the translation of science to action is not happening at the level that it needs to happen.

In the search for effective interventions, a focus on relationships is especially important. These relationships exist between parents and children as well as between care providers and children. They also exist at all ages. For example, the relationships between teenagers and their peers, including boyfriends and girlfriends, can be instrumental in determining the course of their lives. The centrality of relationships raises many questions. For example, should parenting education become universal, and if so how?

It is critical for service providers to meet parents and families where they are in their lives. Existing systems sometimes fail to recognize the circumstances surrounding families and children, especially in cases in which those circumstances have been changing rapidly. Furthermore, these systems face a much greater challenge than just changing the environment. In many cases, they need to change how communities function.

Another issue in the search for effective interventions is the use of evidence. Studies of interventions need to concentrate on the features and approaches of what works, not necessarily on which program or model works. Which features or approaches across programs make for effective interventions? Similarly, randomized control trials have a role in evaluating programs, but more and different kinds of evaluations need to be used to determine the effective aspects of programs. Complementary evaluations that use mixed methods offer a better means of studying programs than the application of a single gold standard. When does an intervention work, for whom, and under what conditions? And how can evaluations be conducted closer to real time so that interventions can be continually monitored and improved?

Today, science is not being used to the extent that it needs to be used to generate new ideas about how to structure and motivate interventions. Scientific findings need to push people's thinking and their commitment to change.

Theme 4: Interactions among early childhood science, policy, and practice are problematic and demand dramatic rethinking.

> Policies and programs aimed at improving the life chances of young children come in many varieties. Some are home based and others are delivered in centers. Some focus on children alone or in groups, and others work primarily with parents. A variety of services have been designed to address the needs of young children whose future prospects are threatened by socioeconomic disadvantages, family disruptions, and diagnosed disabilities. They all share a belief that early childhood development is susceptible to environmental influences and that wise public investments in young children can increase the odds of favorable developmental outcomes. The scientific evidence resoundingly supports these premises. (NRC and IOM, 2000, p. 10)

More than a decade after the release of *From Neurons to Neighborhoods*, many remaining needs in early childhood development can be easily identified. A comprehensive reassessment of the nation's child care and income support policies is needed. Education should recognize and incorporate early learning. The health system needs greater emphasis on prevention and health promotion. The family's role should be more deeply appreciated. A more extended vision is needed for policy, such as the use of Medicaid as a key financing mechanism.

Many of these needs raise the question of whether proposed solutions should be systemic or more targeted. But this is a polarizing way to view what needs to be done. Targeted interventions should be framed within larger systems that are robust, appropriately financed, and universal so that individual programs are not isolated.

A discussion of "systems" is not very accessible to policy makers or the public. A better way of talking about systems is needed so that people can more easily understand what it means to support the child, adolescent, and adult over the lifespan.

In the past, reform efforts have tended to focus on programs rather than systems. A better approach is to focus on quality and outcomes rather than programs. This approach is more realistic in terms of the life of a child and developmental issues. It also would apply to everyone, which would make it more palatable to policy makers.

The state of Colorado has taken such an approach by convening all of the individuals and programs involved in the lives of children and condensing their different visions into a single one-page description. Similarly, the state of Pennsylvania has created benchmarks with appropriate outcomes. For example, teacher certification for K-12 education was restructured so that the same criteria apply to everyone.

State policy and federal policy have quite different functions, and in early childhood development state policy is crucial. The state may be the best place for policy change to occur, and leadership in a state is also essential to policy change.

At the federal level, several concerns exist. Open-ended block grants may be less effective than more directive grants that provide guidelines for what is needed. Funding for early childhood development tends to be scattered, inadequate, and incoherent. Given the burden of bureaucratic costs, would the consolidation of scattered efforts within the federal government provide more money for programs? Or would consolidation make it easier for a program to be pruned or eliminated?

Federal initiatives also have resulted in successes, such as the domestic violence initiative during the Clinton administration. In that case, the Department of Justice and the Department of Health and Human Services worked closely together and made significant progress.

New champions for early childhood development could include philanthropic organizations that are familiar with the science, business leaders, economists, and young entrepreneurs. They could help pave the way for a new overview of the science of early childhood development, which could be called *From Neurons to Neighborhoods to Nations*.

2

Research Issues in Early
Childhood Development

From Neurons to Neighborhoods: The Science of Early Childhood Development had a profound influence on fostering the integration of the science of early childhood development as well as promoting the use of science in early childhood interventions. In many areas the research frontier has progressed far beyond what it was when the report was released. New tools, new concepts, and even new fields of study (such as genomics, epigenetics, and functional neuroimaging) have greatly increased the ability to realize the vision described in *From Neurons to Neighborhoods*.

At the workshop to commemorate the 10th anniversary of the report, three speakers examined specific topics within the diverse array of research areas that constitute the overall science of early childhood development. Alan Guttmacher, Director of the Eunice Kennedy Shriver National Institute of Child Health and Human Development (NICHD), discussed the interdependence of biology and experience in the developing child. Bruce McEwen, Alfred E. Mirsky Professor at Rockefeller University, looked at the exciting work on the biological and neurological consequences of stress. And Deborah Stipek, James Quillen Dean and Professor of Education at Stanford University, discussed emerging work associated with executive functioning in the lives of young children. These three presentations focused on specific areas of research that offer future promise for the continued vitality and promise of developmental science.

NATURE, NURTURE, AND THE RESEARCH AGENDA AT NICHD[1]

Alan Guttmacher
Eunice Kenney Shriver National Institute of
Child Health and Human Development

One of the most influential conclusions of *From Neurons to Neighborhoods* is that it is not nature *or* nurture but nature *and* nurture that matter in early childhood development, said Alan Guttmacher, Director of NICHD. "The acceptance of that today compared to a decade ago is much more pervasive, and that is an important thing."

The acceptance of this thesis has created new opportunities to investigate the complex interactions between nature and nurture that affect early childhood. As an example, Guttmacher cited the National Longitudinal Study of Adolescent Health, which combines longitudinal data on adolescents' social, economic, psychological, and physical well-being with data on family, neighborhood, community, school, friendships, peer groups, and romantic relationships to study how such factors affect health and achievement. He also cited the National Children's Study, which will allow researchers to examine multiple effects of environmental influences and biological factors on the health and development of approximately 100,000 children across the United States from before birth to age 21.

New Research Tools

Recent advances have given researchers new tools to examine early childhood development. In particular, Guttmacher focused on recent advances in genetics, although from an unexpected perspective. "I come here as a certified genomicist to tell you that the real thing we have to focus on is the environment. That's because we have made great strides in the last decade in having tools to look at genetic [influences]. We have not made similar kind of strides in understanding environmental influences."

The sequencing of the human genome has made it possible to identify genes involved in a wide variety of human diseases. For example, new tools and data have made possible investigations known as genome-wide association studies, which began to find genetic variants associated with specific diseases in 2005. Since then, genome-wide association studies have uncovered hundreds of genetic regions involved in human diseases. Guttmacher acknowledged that relatively few of the genetic regions identified so far

---

[1] This section of the chapter is based on the presentation by Alan Guttmacher titled "The Federal Policy Perspective" at *From Neurons to Neighborhoods* Anniversary: Ten Years Later.

appear to be involved in human behavior or cognition, but many of the diseases associated with these genetic variants are relevant to early childhood.

However, uncovering the environmental factors that contribute to human diseases—much less human behaviors—is much more difficult. Furthermore, changing outcomes for children will involve changing their environments, not their genes. "To understand this complex interaction, we need to understand environment *and* genetics," he said.

Geneticists have always assumed that genes influence behavior, but a growing body of evidence indicates that behavior influences genes in ways that were not anticipated. In particular, experiences are able to change genetic activity that once was assumed to be hard-wired. The new field of epigenetics, for example, is examining how experiences act on the configuration and modifications of the DNA molecule to affect the activities of genes. These are "examples of the kinds of things we should be thinking about," said Guttmacher.

An important focus of research will be to understand individual variation in learning. In the past, geneticists have tended to divide people into categories, but everyone is biologically unique in terms of genome and experiences. This research will include the use of new neuroimaging techniques to explore variation in learning, longitudinal studies of learning that look at the interaction of genetic variation and sociocultural influences, examination of how or if early learning experiences modify the child's genome through epigenetic modification, and the application of new research knowledge to improve early interventions for individuals with learning disabilities.

Another important research focus will be neural plasticity—how neuronal structure and function change in response to experiences. For example, how are neural circuits reconfigured as a result of experience? What are the environmental experiences necessary for normal or optimal development in various sensitive periods of neurocognitive development? How can the rehabilitation and adaptation of function contribute to recovery from disease or injury?

The Research Agenda at NICHD

NICHD launched a year-long process to identify scientific opportunities over the next decade across the institute's mission, which includes pediatric health, maternal health, rehabilitation medicine, and many other topics. The aim, said Guttmacher, is to develop a scientific vision that sets an ambitious agenda and inspires the institute, the research community, and the institute's partners to achieve critical scientific goals and meet pressing public health needs.

NICHD will hold workshops to gather input from external experts, commission white papers for workshops to create a foundation for the vision, convene a large multidisciplinary meeting to shape emerging plans, and welcome public input throughout the process. The target date for publishing the vision is December 2011. (For more information, see http://www.nichd.nih.gov/vision.)

The institute's staff has identified nine scientific themes to be explored in workshops:

- Behavior
- Cognition
- Development
- Developmental origins of health and disease
- Diagnostics and therapeutics
- Environment
- Plasticity
- Pregnancy and pregnancy outcomes
- Reproduction

At least seven of these themes apply directly to early childhood development, said Guttmacher.

In addition, a number of topics cut across all of these themes:

- Analytical and measurement tools and methods
- Animal and computational models
- Bioethics
- Bioinformatics
- Biotechnologies and bioengineering, including high-throughput, assistive, and related technologies
- Developmental trajectories
- Differences and disparities across populations
- Epigenetics and metagenomics
- Functional status
- Global health
- Implementation science, including health economics
- Nutrition
- Preventive and personalized medicine
- Stem cells
- Systems biology
- Training and mentoring

The intention is to produce a research agenda that is useful not only to NICHD but also to many other organizations that are interested in early childhood development, said Guttmacher. In this way, research will be able to inform policy through investigations of the interactions between biology and experience in early childhood. The overall result will be to improve children's outcomes through the application of new tools and approaches.

Discussion

During the discussion period, Guttmacher was asked how NICHD can overcome the disciplinary barriers that impede needed research on early childhood development. He replied that the program review currently under way at the institute is organized around broad themes, not around existing disciplines, to conceptualize the research agenda in a broader way. Disciplinary boundaries are a problem for the National Institutes of Health (NIH) in general, he noted. "No matter what area of health and development one is talking about at NIH, [disciplinary] silos don't tend to correlate with biology in the real world." The challenge for transdisciplinary research is to overcome these silos both scientifically and programmatically. The program staff at NIH take great pride in their grantees and the fields they support. But this pride also can breed narrow thinking. "In academia we tend to identify with certain systems and certain programs," he said. "We need to think more creatively. For instance, if you think about the environmental-genetics construct, the only way to do that research is if we have people who are world-class experts in both of those worlds."

Training is one way to resolve this problem. "I would hope that we would train folks who are comfortable across this broad swath of knowledge," he said. "Right now we don't have those people. We need more creative ways of bringing teams together." He noted that a historical strength of the IOM and the NRC is their ability to bring together people with very different perspectives—as the title *From Neurons to Neighborhoods* suggests. More of that kind of audacity is needed in the scientific community.

NICHD also needs to hear from and listen to the users of its research, Guttmacher said. This input relates both to the scientific opportunities and to the public health impact of research. A sense of the key questions that can be answered would be extremely useful to NICHD. Partnerships between agencies involved in policies and programs also can yield such input. Such partnerships can lead to experiments that reveal whether novel interventions are having a desired effect, so long as these effects are accurately measured.

THE ROLE OF STRESS IN PHYSICAL AND MENTAL HEALTH[2]

Bruce McEwen
Rockefeller University

People's biological reactions to stress are a good example of the interplay between biology and the environment, said Bruce McEwen, Alfred E. Mirsky Professor at Rockefeller University. Roughly speaking, stress can be divided into three categories. *Positive stress* can be generated by a personal challenge, in which satisfactorily meeting that challenge gives rise to a sense of mastery and control. Positive stress points toward the existence of a healthy brain architecture, self-esteem, good judgment, and impulse control.

Tolerable stress results from the occurrence of adverse life events that are buffered by supportive relationships. The result of such stress is coping and recovery, again suggesting the presence of healthy brain architecture, self-esteem, good judgment, and impulse control along with good external supports.

Toxic stress results from unbuffered adverse events that are extended and/or sizable. The result is poor coping and compromised recovery. For children, the consequences of toxic stress include lifelong risk for physical and mental disorders, which is likely to be due to compromised brain architecture and dysregulated physiological systems.

The brain is the central organ in the stress response, including adaptation. The brain perceives and judges what is threatening and therefore stressful. In this way, the brain determines the subsequent responses to stress, including adaptation. The term "allostasis" refers to the physiological process of producing hormones in the body that produce a reaction to stress. The term "allostatic load" refers to the cumulative burden on the body as a result of stress and harmful health behaviors resulting from a stressful life.

There are many types of stressors, including trauma, abuse, major life events, family conflict, workplace environments, and community factors. In addition, each person has a unique response to stress determined by genetics, early developmental history, and experiences throughout life.

Stress causes the release of hormones in the brain that travel to other parts of the body, which in turn cause subsequent hormonal responses and other physiological reactions. In some cases, these hormones have beneficial effects. For example, in the short term, these hormones can

---

[2] This section of the chapter is based on the presentation by Bruce McEwen titled "Implications for Physical and Mental Health" at *From Neurons to Neighborhoods* Anniversary: Ten Years Later.

enhance immune responses, memory, energy replenishment, and cardiovascular function. But if stress is prolonged or severe, these same hormones can cause harmful inflammatory and immune responses, impair memory, elevate mineral loss from bones and muscle wasting, and contribute to metabolic syndrome. In addition, other physiological reactions can disrupt brain, metabolic, immune, and cardiovascular function, creating a complex and nonlinear network of stress responses.

The brain also governs behavioral responses. For example, it can react to stress through fighting or fleeing. It can motivate personal behaviors that cause adverse outcomes like eating too much, drinking too much, not getting enough sleep, or not engaging in health-promoting behaviors like regular physical activity. The behavioral responses encompassed by the term "lifestyle" are also important, because they can influence the allostatic load (see Figure 2-1).

Finally, toxic chemicals in the environment can feed into the network of allostasis. For example, toxicants in the environment can increase inflammatory responses, which in turn can increase hormonal secretion and create imbalances in the allostatic network.

Diseases exacerbated by the allostatic network include cardiovascular disease, depression, diabetes, Alzheimer's disease, arthritis, and cancer. All are diseases of modern life, McEwen pointed out, and many others could be included.

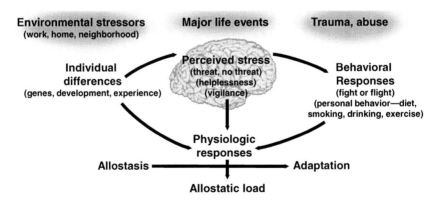

FIGURE 2-1 The brain plays a central role in mediating between a person's experiences and physiological reactions, including the stress reaction.
SOURCE: Reprinted from McEwen, B. S. 1998. Protective and damaging effects of stress mediators. *New England Journal of Medicine* 338(3):171-179. Copyright 1998 with permission from Bruce McEwen.

Stress and Brain Plasticity

The brain is capable of considerable remodeling, even in adults, McEwen observed. For example, the dendrites that receive electrical impulses from other nerve cells and then help pass them on to others can grow or shrink throughout life. The synapses through which nerve cells communicate with each other also can change as a result of experience. The brain can even form new neurons in particular brain regions such as the hippocampus, which plays a key role in certain kinds of memory. In fact, particular kinds of stress suppress the generation of new neurons, and the regulation of this process is thought to be a key factor in depressive illnesses.

Research on animals and, to a more limited extent, imaging techniques in humans have shown that stress can cause neurons to shrink or grow. For example, in the hippocampus, stress can cause neurons to shrink, so that dendritic networks become simplified. But in a part of the region called the basal lateral amygdala, which is critical in memories of fear, stress causes an expansion of the dendritic tree. Similar processes can occur in a cortical area called the orbital frontal cortex, which is involved in determining the salience of reward or punishment, and in the medial prefrontal cortex, which has important roles in decision making, working memory, and top-down control of mood, anxiety, and autonomic and neuroendocrine functions. "What you have is growth in some areas, shrinkage in some areas," said McEwen. "Some parts of the brain become more activated and more responsive. Others become less responsive."

The good news is that animal models have produced some evidence that the brain can recover when the stress ends, so "this is not an example of brain damage per se."

The Origins of Adult Diseases

Many adult diseases have their origins in adverse events early in a child's life (Shonkoff et al., 2009). Studies have shown, for example, that living in a chaotic home can lead to greater helplessness and distress, poor self-regulatory behaviors, and perhaps deficits in prefrontal cortical function. Other studies have documented elevated levels of obesity, blood pressure, cardiovascular reactivity, and systematic inflammation as well as poor dental health as a result of chaotic home situations in early childhood, leading to shorter average lifespans (Brown et al., 2009). Adverse childhood experiences can exacerbate obesity, illicit drug use, mental health problems, sexual and reproductive health issues, and general health and social problems. Low socioeconomic status is associated with poor language skills, poor executive function, and other effects on learning ability. Maltreatment of children has a cascade of consequences that influence cognitive and in-

CASCADE OF CONSEQUENCES

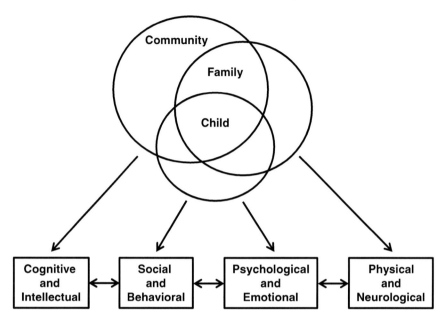

FIGURE 2-2 The experiences that a child has as part of a family and a community have a cascade of consequences for biological and neurological functioning. SOURCE: McEwen, 2010.

tellectual ability, social and behavioral skills, psychological and emotional processes, and physical and neurological functions (see Figure 2-2).

Animal models have played a large role in studying the physiological effects of the environment. For example, in rodent models prenatal stress retards the development of the hippocampus, whereas good maternal care improves the emotional state and even seems to affect the lifespan of offspring. With a background of good maternal care, novel experiences can benefit cognitive and social development in rodent models. Similarly, studies of rhesus monkeys have shown that maternal anxiety can be transmitted to offspring. And animal research is showing that the intrauterine environment has immense importance not only for things like metabolism and obesity but also for behavior.

The new field of epigenetics is looking at gene–environment interactions that have physiological and behavioral consequences, including the effects of stress. Epigenetic modifications to DNA include the actions of proteins called histones that determine the folding or unfolding of DNA to expose or hide genes, the binding of protein regulators to DNA and the addition of methyl groups to DNA that influence gene expression, and the production of small RNA molecules that regulate the survival and translation of messenger RNAs. Some of these effects can be passed from one generation to the next and influence such traits as obesity and parental behavior. McEwen observed: "To reduce the obesity epidemic, for example—which by the way has effects on cognitive function as well as other diseases—we have to deal with nutrition, stress, and other things in families expecting children. We can't just start after the child is born."

In these ways, the experiences people have during their life become embedded in their brains and in their physiological reactions to events. Heavy allostatic loads, for example, can alter and sensitize the brain and the body to respond in certain ways to similar experiences. Experiences involving the stress response also can have positive consequences. For example, regular physical activity demonstrably improves executive function. "We all know that getting up and walking around helps to jog our cognitive function. That is a very simple and direct solution to help a lot of people help themselves, and particularly kids."

The centrality of the stress response means that interventions to decrease stress and the harmful effects of stress can produce major benefits for society. For example, interventions influencing early childhood development can produce major financial returns through increased earnings to individuals, lower crime rates, savings on special education and welfare, and increased income tax revenues (Center on the Developing Child at Harvard University, 2010a). "The returns on investment . . . are significant and important," said McEwen, "besides the fact that it is the right thing to do."

Discussion

During the discussion session, McEwen pointed out that top-down policy directives need attention, in addition to bottom-up interventions. Government policies and work-related policies of private enterprise that affect how families and children live are essentially health policies. Therefore, policies and health interventions need to work in tandem. "Societal change takes a long time and requires a political process," he said. Specific programs can be the consequence of overarching policies, he said, citing the Nurse Family Partnership, the Perry Preschool Project, and the Abecedarian Project. A combined approach "is the most important way of dealing with things," he continued.

Policy makers and the public need to know how the brain is involved in early learning and development. In particular, McEwen mentioned that the Society for Neuroscience is organizing a public outreach effort on early childhood development to capture the attention of the public and policy makers.

WHAT WE HAVE LEARNED ABOUT LEARNING[3]

Deborah Stipek
Stanford University

From Neurons to Neighborhoods provided incontrovertible evidence for several key conclusions, said Deborah Stipek, James Quillen Dean and Professor of Education at Stanford University. It showed that children's experiences shape the architecture of their brains as well as their functioning. It also demonstrated the value of early interventions, including high-quality early childhood education.

These conclusions inevitably raise questions about leverage points in the lives of young children. An especially important question is, What domains of early skills can be used to enhance later skill development? The task is complicated by the interdependence of skills. For example, when children who are less prepared enter school, they lack not just academic skills. They also tend to be behind other children in social, emotional, and cognitive skills. These dimensions are highly interactive, Stipek observed, and each contains many subdimensions.

The question then becomes whether to intervene along all of these dimensions or to direct attention to particular dimensions that leverage other kinds of skills. "How [can] a skill that you develop at the age of 3 contribute to the kinds of academic demands that you are expected to meet at the age of 5 or 6 or 8 or 11?" she asked.

Stipek argued that interventions in particular domains can act as particularly effective leverage points, noting that "Piaget taught us that cognitive development is a system of understandings, and that changes in any part of that system are likely to influence changes in other parts of the system." As examples of potentially important leverage points, she discussed verbal skills, social skills, mathematical skills, and the executive functions that underlie many developing skills in young children.

Verbal Skills

The verbal input that children receive—both in terms of the number of words and the number of different words they hear—has a strong correlation with their vocabulary, Stipek observed. Verbal learning also exhibits a reciprocal loop. As children develop better vocabulary and literacy skills, their executive functions are enhanced. For example, recent research has

---

[3] This section of the chapter is based on the presentation by Deborah Stipek titled "Implications for Motivation and Learning" at *From Neurons to Neighborhoods* Anniversary: Ten Years Later.

shown that the verbal environment of children even in infancy predicts their working memory, their processing speed, and their underlying cognitive skills, which in turn predict their vocabulary development. In addition, the levels of skill children have when they enter school influence the kinds of educational environments they experience. These skill levels influence teachers' expectations for the kind of work they can do and help determine which other students they are grouped with in classrooms.

Because of these effects, verbal input has a multiplicative influence on children's lives. "I would propose that the verbal environment might be one of those leverage points that we need to take a look at," said Stipek.

Social Skills

Social skills also predict learning. Children's ability to get along with peers, their skills at interacting socially, and the absence of aggressive or disruptive behavior are believed to facilitate their learning. Similarly, the relationships that children form are important predictors of how well they learn, and they learn better when they have a secure and caring adult available to them.

Research in the past decade has begun to explore these connections more thoroughly. For example, increased aggression has been shown in children who are having difficulty learning to read. In this situation, learning predicts social skills better than social skills predict learning. This does not imply that social skills are unimportant, Stipek emphasized, but the common assumption that social skills cause academic skills needs further analysis. The research suggests that improving academic skills may serve as a lever for promoting positive social behavior.

Mathematical Skills

The development of mathematical skills has been part of childhood since antiquity, but these skills are relatively new to preschool. Stipek and her colleagues have had to visit preschools multiple times to find any evidence of mathematical activities. "It is something that has been neglected," she said, "but recent evidence suggests that it may deserve more attention than we have been giving it." A recent report by the National Research Council (2009) highlighted research in this area.

A recent study compared literacy and mathematics skills for children entering kindergarten to predict their skills in reading and mathematics in third grade. The mathematical entry skills were much stronger predictors of both mathematical and reading skills in third grade than were reading entry skills. The reasons for this correlation remain unclear. Does learning in mathematics facilitate later thinking skills and the ability to perform in school, or do early mathematical skills reflect some underlying executive functions that influence learning? "We [don't] really know," said Stipek, "but data like this suggest we better find out . . . because mathematics might be much more important than we have thought."

Research also has demonstrated that young children are more capable of learning mathematics than was previously believed. They can do much more than just "macaroni math"—gluing three macaronis in one box and five in another. They can learn to use numbers to describe order and measure, to use patterns to recognize relationships, and to use geometry to represent objects. "There is a lot to mathematics even for young children," Stipek observed.

The natural progression of mathematical understanding is fairly well understood, she said, as are effective strategies to teach mathematics to young children, and research-based preschool mathematics curricula exist. Stipek observed, "It is not that we don't have the tools, but we have not been convinced of the value of mathematics." If this is a productive leverage point, as current research suggests it might be, teachers and caregivers will need to develop skills to help children develop fundamental mathematical skills.

Executive Functions

As a final example of a potential leverage point, Stipek spoke more broadly about executive functions (see Figure 2-3). Research has shown that executive functions are important for social skills as well as learning. For example, studies that hold constant aspects of executive functions, such as attention and impulsivity, no longer detect a relationship between aggression and academic performance, which suggests that executive functions may be critical in both domains. In social interactions, children need to be able to remember the rules of the game. They need to inhibit the impulse to push a child out of the way when they run for a ball or to grab a toy that they want. They need to plan strategies for entering play or for engaging other kids in play. Inhibitory control, emotional self-regulation, memory, attention—which are all executive functions—are all important in social interactions as well as intellectual work.

As an example, Stipek cited a classroom of preschoolers in which a teacher asks a question. Every child raises his or her hand, but when the teacher calls on someone, that child has no idea what to say. "This is an example of poor inhibitory control," said Stipek. They want to participate so they raise their hand, but they have not thought through the fact that they do not have an answer. "We see these executive functions play out on the playground in a social context and in the classroom all the time."

In intellectual work, children need to remember instructions. They need

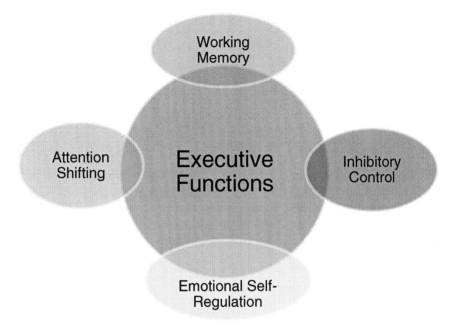

FIGURE 2-3 Executive functions include both cognitive and emotional skills and attributes.
SOURCE: Stipek, 2010.

to be able to pay attention to the task at hand despite distractions. They need to be able to shift their attention if the strategy they are using does not seem to be working. They need to inhibit the immediate action that comes to mind and consider alternatives.

Researchers need to study executive functions to learn more about how they influence behavior in both the learning context and the social context, Stipek said. Today very few interventions that target executive functions are available, despite their potential value in building childhood skills.

Effective Interventions

The evidence on leverage points in the lives of young children supports the need for effective interventions. A strong foundation "influences children's opportunities and abilities to learn from the very first year of their life," said Stipek. The existing evidence does not necessarily indicate exactly where to intervene, but it identifies questions that deserve much more attention.

Intervening in the lives of young children is inevitably complex. Young children are learning language (and sometimes additional languages in addition to their native language), pre-literacy skills, social and emotional skills, impulse control, and many other skills. They are developing relationships with parents, caregivers, educators, and other adults. People who have major responsibility for young children need much more support and training to guide development in the face of this daunting complexity.

Several outstanding questions have important implications for the research needed to prepare for future updating of *From Neurons to Neighborhoods*, said Stipek. First, the interconnections between skills need to be better understood. How do interventions in one area affect skills in other domains? For example, very few researchers assessing the effects of interventions targeting either academic or social skills have assessed the effects of the intervention on the other domain. She expressed her view: "I strongly recommend that we look at these cross-domain effects. It will help us to understand the interconnections among domains of development and to identify those important leverage points."

Researchers also need to develop a better understanding of what kinds of skills teachers and caregivers need and how to provide them with those skills. The focus on credentials such as academic degrees can detract from the important questions: What do people need to know and be able to do and how can these skills be developed?

The only way to convince policy makers of the need to invest in early childhood development is to convince the public, Stipek concluded. Advocates need to start where people's hearts are, which is with their own children. They need to understand that "their child's future depends as much on other people's children's future as on their own child's future. And if they want their child to thrive, they need to make sure that they are promoting and supporting the welfare of the people [working with] their child," she noted.

Discussion

Stipek was asked during the discussion session how executive functions can be measured in preschoolers. She commented that for many domains of development there is a confusing array of overlapping and differently named measures. Stipek had begun compiling a list of measures of learning-related behaviors, but quit when she reached 30 measures. One of the things the field needs to do, she said, is develop greater consensus about the conceptualization and measurement of different domains of development.

Stipek also was asked how to provide incentives to draw the best minds into teaching young children. She answered that people need to be paid more. Care providers are not going to sacrifice the needs of their own families to care for other children. "We are going to have to increase pay. That to me is a no-brainer," she observed.

Specific interventions also bear promise. For example, a program at Stanford called Jumpstart gives students a year-long seminar in early childhood education along with 6 hours per week spent in a low-income community working with preschool children. "These bright, energetic undergraduates are totally hooked by the time they finish the year," Stipek said, "if they are not going into early childhood education, many of them end up going into K-12 education." However, they will not stay in early childhood education unless their pay and the respect they are accorded by the rest of society improves. In countries that compare favorably to the United States in educational performance, educators are paid well relative to other professions and education is a highly respected profession. "We don't have that in the United States," Stipek said. "Partly it is because people underestimate the difficulty. They think that [working with] young children is babysitting. They do not understand the many interconnected domains of development that teachers need to understand and promote, especially if we want to close the achievement gap."

3

Policy Issues in Early
Childhood Development

One of the distinctive features of the science of early childhood development is the extent to which research findings evolve under the anxious and eager eyes of millions of families, policy makers, and service providers who seek authoritative guidance as they address the challenges of promoting the health and well-being of young children. Moreover, as a public issue, questions about effective practices in the care and protection of children confront basic traditional values in areas that include personal responsibility, individual self-reliance, and the role of government involvement in people's lives.

Many policies have changed at the federal and state level since the initial publication of *From Neurons to Neighborhoods*, some because of the scientific advances catalyzed by the report. More emphasis is placed upon early childhood education than it was a decade ago. State and federal maternal health legislation has expanded to include home visiting programs throughout the states. The Special Supplemental Nutrition Program for Women, Infants, and Children (WIC) has moved away from formulas toward packages for providing food for families. At the same time, socioeconomic and demographic trends have created new challenges, with a greater percentage of children growing up in poverty and to foreign-born mothers.

Three speakers at the workshop to commemorate the 10th anniversary of *From Neurons to Neighborhoods* examined public policy issues related to the report and raised questions about future directions that deserve attention. Joan Lombardi, Deputy Assistant Secretary and Interdepartmental Liaison for Early Childhood Development in the U.S. Department of Health and Human Services, described changes in federal policies affecting young children and families over the past decade and the role of the science base in contributing to those changes. Mary Eming Young, Lead Child Development Specialist for the World Bank's Human Development Network, spoke about how to mobilize science to promote policy innovation from an international perspective. Jack Shonkoff, Director of the Center on the Developing Child at Harvard University, presented a new framework in examining how the science of early childhood development can contribute to social change.

THE FEDERAL POLICY ENVIRONMENT[1]

Joan Lombardi
U.S. Department of Health and Human Services

Before the workshop, Joan Lombardi, Deputy Assistant Secretary and Interdepartmental Liaison for Early Childhood Development in the U.S. Department of Health and Human Services, asked several people for their impression of the report *From Neurons to Neighborhoods*. One described it as a graduate school course condensed into a single book. Another said it was the embodiment of the importance of early childhood. A third observed that it affirmed the importance of the work they were doing. "We can't underscore enough the importance of [this] report," Lombardi said.

In her talk, Lombardi described the evolution of the federal policy environment and its relation to the early childhood science base. *From Neurons to Neighborhoods* emphasized several key scientific concepts:

- Biology and experience are both important in early childhood development.
- Context shapes the developing child.
- The growth of self-regulation is a cornerstone of early childhood development across domains of behavior.
- Relationships are the building blocks of human development.
- Vulnerability and resilience are key features of childhood and can be affected by both risk factors and protective factors.
- The course of development can be altered in early childhood by effective interventions.

These concepts have had great staying power and continue to influence federal policy today, Lombardi said.

---

[1] This section of the chapter is based on the presentation by Joan Lombardi titled "The Federal Policy Perspective" at *From Neurons to Neighborhoods* Anniversary: Ten Years Later.

The Policy Context

In *From Neurons to Neighborhoods*, the Committee on Integrating the Science of Early Childhood Development pointed to five ongoing transformations affecting families with young children:

1. Changes in the nature, schedule, and amount of work engaged in by parents of young children.
2. More children spending time in child care of varying quality starting at a young age.
3. Continuing high levels of economic hardships among families even in a strong economy.
4. Increasing cultural diversity and the persistence of disparities among subgroups.
5. Greater awareness of the effects of stress on young children.

One of the most important points the report made is that the effects of these changes should not be viewed in isolation, Lombardi said. Development is an integrated process. Similarly, federal policies that affect early childhood education should be seen as an integrated system. These policies encompass health, mental health, nutrition, child care, education, family support, and child protection (see Figure 3-1). Many federal policies in these areas are long-standing and have had an important effect on the lives of families. "We do have things to celebrate in the policy arena," said Lombardi.

Policies that fall outside what is traditionally seen as early childhood concerns also have a substantial influence on children and families, including housing, economic, and transportation policies. "These are the things that I hear about when I travel across the country as having a profound effect on families," said Lombardi.

During the decade before the release of *From Neurons to Neighborhoods*, a robust set of early childhood policies emerged, including policies influencing child care, family and medical leave, Early Head Start, welfare reform, child support, the Children's Health Insurance Program, and family preservation. It was not a perfect agenda, Lombardi noted. "We didn't get it right in each one of those places. But we moved the needle, and we moved it in a bipartisan way."

In the decade since the report was released, the policy environment has shifted. At the federal level, policy changes have emphasized literacy, assessment, welfare reform, and family structure, although significant resources to back these changes have become available only in the past 2 years with the passage of the American Recovery and Reinvestment Act and the Patient Protection and Affordable Care Act. During this same period,

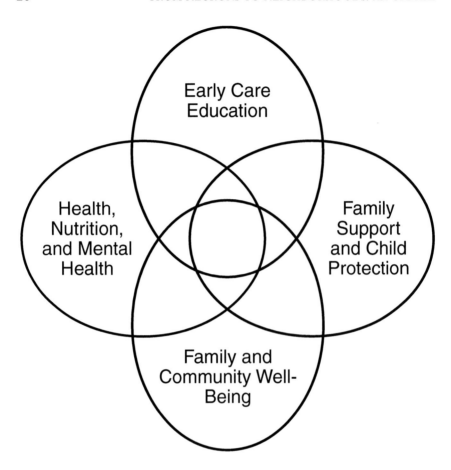

FIGURE 3-1 Public policies that affect early childhood development collectively overlap.
SOURCE: Lombardi, 2010.

the states have been laboratories of innovation. For example, the expansion of prekindergarten programs at the state level was an enormous step forward, said Lombardi.

However, the rate of children ages 0 to 5 living in poverty also has increased over the past decade, and the fraction of young children living in poverty is greater than the fraction of poor children ages 6 to 17. "Unfortunately the line is going in the wrong direction," Lombardi said. "That is a concern for all of us."

New Policy Developments

Recent federal policy changes have brought new attention to early childhood, with a particular emphasis on prenatal care to age 8. The Patient Protection and Affordable Care Act included authorization for the Maternal, Infant, and Early Childhood Home Visiting Program, which will make "an important difference to young children, particularly young children at risk," according to Lombardi. New research initiatives include a study of the workforce for early childhood care conducted through the National Academies. Child Care, Head Start, and Early Head Start programs have all been expanded. In general, trends in the development of policy include emphases on evidence, place, and prevention.

These changes reflect a gradual shift from a diverse set of programs to a more systematic approach, Lombardi observed. At the state level, advisory councils are coordinating programs. State and federal programs are moving toward more integrated standards. Common governance and professional development across programs are being emphasized. Families are being engaged in new ways, so that they can be more systematically involved in their children's health, learning, and development. Data systems are being created at the individual and public health levels to track developmental measures across childhood and adolescence.

Reflecting these changes, the U.S. Department of Health and Human Services has created new linkages with the U.S. Department of Education. An interagency policy board created by the two departments is beginning to align policies systematically. "It is an honor," said Lombardi, "to be working for an administration and a President who understand that learning begins at birth and that investments in health and education have a profound impact on development."

Implications for the Research Agenda

As part of this new emphasis on early childhood development, a robust agenda is emerging at the federal level and in partnership with states and communities, according to Lombardi. She posed four questions to the research community that have significant policy relevance:

1. What are the key elements that lead to improved child health and developmental outcomes in early childhood programs?
2. How can gains be sustained over time, and how does one program build on another?
3. How can the impact of community-wide strategies be evaluated?
4. What is the impact of media and technology on young children and family relationships?

Implications for the Policy Agenda

The policy agenda remains unfinished. *From Neurons to Neighborhoods* began to fill the gap between what is known and what is being done, but the gap remains large. Lombardi suggested emphasizing the effects of policy on primary caregivers because of their significance to children. "They need time, information, and social networks of support," she said. As a new grandmother, Lombardi added, she has been struck by how little time parents have with young children from the earliest ages and how little support they receive.

Another important policy focus is to link child welfare more directly to early childhood, particularly with an increasing number of very young children in the foster care and child protection system. Quality early childhood services can be an important respite for families and a supportive environment for the developing child.

Early childhood mental health programs need to be taken to scale, according to Lombardi. The Substance Abuse and Mental Health Services Administration has launched several important demonstration projects, and these need to be expanded, she said.

Child care should not be seen as creating deficits in children but as an opportunity to provide quality services to them. Much needs to be done to provide quality across child care and other early childhood programs. In particular, children from low-income families need access to quality services. "Federal child care assistance is still serving only 1 of 6 eligible children. That is not good enough."

Good policies also incorporate consideration of the life cycle. Early childhood development is linked to youth development, and both are linked to adult development.

Finally, much can be learned from policies, research, programs, and experiences in other countries, and countries with proportionately greater needs require higher levels of attention and support. "Along with sharing research, we should be focusing much more attention on the millions and millions of children around the world who may be surviving but are not thriving because of malnutrition, violence, and poverty," said Lombardi. "It is time for us to step up to the plate and continue to invest in those children."

Policy debates in recent years have tended to pit personal responsibility against public policies. *From Neurons to Neighborhoods* said that the time has come to move beyond such either/ors. Lombardi concluded her remarks by quoting from the report: "In the final analysis, healthy child development is dependent on a combination of individual responsibility, informal social supports, and formalized structures that evolve within a society."

Discussion

A questioner asked Lombardi about the advantages of place-based policies compared with traditional health or human service systems, and Lombardi responded that she views the two as inseparable. "What you do in a community is pull all those pieces together." For example, a major problem in the existing network of services is a lack of investment in the early childhood workforce, particularly for infants and toddlers. "It takes time and multiple service providers working together in a community to make that change. It is not a simple fix." Only team efforts will be able to make changes of the necessary magnitude.

There is a tremendous need, said Lombardi during the discussion period, to bridge the gap between the research community and what is going on in actual programs. Important innovations are occurring in early childhood development. Programs serving very young children are reaching very different types of families even as the demographics of American families change rapidly. Practitioners have wisdom and evidence that will lead to better research questions and better policies, and both research results and policy decisions will be easier to communicate if researchers and policymakers interact directly with people who are doing the work.

A GLOBAL PERSPECTIVE[2]

Mary Eming Young
The World Bank

Just as *From Neurons to Neighborhoods* led to major early childhood initiatives in the United States, the global community has been converging on the importance of early childhood development and the need for urgent action. These calls for action have several sources, said Mary Eming Young, Lead Child Development Specialist for the World Bank's Human Development Network. International and regional agencies such as the World Bank, the United Nations, the Inter-American Development Bank, and the Asian Development Bank have been supporting early childhood development programs through advocacy, funding, and technical assistance. For example, the recent report *Closing the Gap in a Generation: Health Equity Through Action on the Social Determinants of Health* from the World Health Organization observes that the healthy development of young children is a powerful equalizer for all nations (Commission on Social Determinants

---

[2] This section of the chapter is based on the presentation by Mary Eming Young titled "Lessons Learned from Global Perspective" at *From Neurons to Neighborhoods* Anniversary: Ten Years Later.

of Health, 2008). In addition, such academic journals as the *Lancet* have published major articles on early childhood development (Engle et al., 2007; Grantham-McGregor et al., 2007; Jolly, 2007; Walker et al., 2007). And regional initiatives in such areas as Latin America have given highest priority to early childhood development programs as both a short-term and a long-term solution for addressing poverty.

Three key messages have emerged from these calls for action, stated Young. First, start at the beginning—that is, integrate healthy childhood development into prenatal, early health, and parent education services. Second, get ready for success—that is, ensure children's access to services before they enter school, beginning with the most vulnerable and disadvantaged children. Third, include early childhood in all national policy plans across sectors.

Closing the Gap

Despite the recent global emphasis on early childhood development, much remains to be done to close the gap between understanding and action, said Young. Especially in developing countries, the science of early childhood development still needs to be translated into large-scale programs for young children.

Young identified three obstacles to action. First, the time between making a change and realizing the benefits can be protracted. Policy makers must understand that they need to invest in early childhood education now for payoffs to occur later. Also, children, and especially the poor, do not have a political voice or representation to defend their interests.

Second, the complexity of early childhood development demands an integrated approach that encompasses all levels and sectors of society. Today the health, education, and social protection sectors tend to work in silos. They do not work together to identify and pursue coordinated and practical approaches to child development. But no single sector can solve the problem on its own.

Third, the necessary infrastructure for early childhood development needs to be built from the bottom up. Throughout the world, early childhood development programs are uniquely dependent on a complex network of local, regional, and national institutions for financial management and implementation. Say that early childhood development programs consist of thousands of micro projects that serve 15 to 20 children each, Young observed. Clusters of 15 to 20 micro projects would form neighborhood clusters. These neighborhood clusters would depend on parent associations for organizational support, such as establishing contracts with local providers, lobbying local authorities, or networking with volunteer organizations. Neighborhood clusters in turn would depend on city- or district-wide support systems. The aim of all these networks would be to strengthen the basic unit of society—the family. But communities cannot take on this task successfully without strong public policies.

As an indication of the scale of the challenge, Young cited the Head Start program's coverage of about 1 million children in the United States, which is about half of the intended beneficiaries. Yet, approximately 200 million children worldwide are estimated to be at risk of poor development, and this figure is underestimated because it uses a poverty rate of less than $1 dollar a day of family income to determine if a child is at risk.

An Agenda for the Next Decade

Young identified four main tasks for the next decade.

The first is to rigorously foster global understanding and awareness of the importance of early childhood development. Specifically, it is critical to communicate the importance of healthy brain development in early childhood for the overall health, well-being, and competence of populations. This knowledge needs to spread to all people at every level and especially to parents, caregivers, communities, government policy makers, financiers, and heads of states. The creation and strengthening of national policies affecting early childhood development depend on awareness of its importance, yet the tipping point for many necessary actions has not been reached.

The second task is to promote a transdisciplinary science of human development that combines the natural and social sciences. New and developing fields such as neuroscience and epigenetics could provide the basis for research and the application of that research across all disciplines, including the health sciences and the social sciences.

The third task is to expand access to early childhood development programs and ensure the quality of these programs. Enhanced professional development and better understanding of the minimal requirements for quality will strengthen programs. Identifying what works and what does not work will lead to better design and scale-up of cost-effective options. The private sector needs incentives to invest in early childhood development. A particular need is for understanding governance at the macro level—what are the rules of the game, the laws, the attitudes, and the social structures that affect policies toward early childhood development?

The fourth task is to assess the effects of early childhood development programs systematically and comparatively. Databases of child outcomes with and without programs are needed, and using the children's outcomes could then be benchmarked using these databases. Useful databases would range far beyond small-scale research evaluations. Benchmarks are crucial for informing policy makers about where, how, and which programs to scale up and for attaining universality, accountability, and comparability within and among countries.

Young observed that, in public health systems, children's health and well-being are largely measured by negative outcomes such as pathology, mortality, or low birth weight instead of positive outcomes such as well-being or competence. In education, measures focus on children's access to school, enrollment rates, or educational failures. Measurement of learning outcomes often comes near the end of compulsory education, which is too late, Young said. Such assessments fail to recognize the issues in the early years that set the trajectory for later learning and performance. Assessment tools and measures need to encompass the whole child and be multidimensional reflections of cognitive, social, or emotional development. They also need to be applicable to groups of children, not just to individual children, Young said.

By speaking in a common language about the transdisciplinary dimensions of early human development and by gathering best practices from countries that have implemented coherent and comprehensive sets of social policies toward early childhood development, the machinery of public policy can be leveraged to improve the lives of children around the world.

Discussion

In response to a question about the key skills needed by the early childhood workforce in developing countries, Young observed that caregivers and providers need an understanding of developmentally appropriate practices. An area that cuts across all ages is the importance of relationships in providing quality care. In the past, considerable attention has focused on the curriculum provided in early childhood education. But a more important bottom line is quality. From home-based programs to formal education, the quality of the interactions between adults and children fosters learning and development.

Young also was asked whether experiences in developing countries have lessons for the United States, and she observed that a great deal can be learned from developing countries. For example, Brazil, Cuba, Mexico, and other Latin American countries have made great progress establishing a continuum of programs beginning with prenatal care and extending through primary school. They are harnessing new understandings from science to build parenting and early childhood programs. And political leaders are recognizing that early childhood development needs to be part of their political platforms to be elected.

In response to a question about how best to build capacity for early childhood development, Young emphasized transdisciplinary training for everyone involved with the field, from parents and care providers to researchers and policy makers.

One questioner pointed out that political conflict and violence pose huge barriers to healthy child development, which caused Young to reiterate the need to start early. Children in conflict-burdened states have an even greater need of nurturing, nutrition, and stimulation. "For us to have tolerant, pluralistic societies, we need to start earlier," she observed. Young quoted a former minister of education who was also a pediatrician who told her that investing in early childhood development is a matter of national security; her comment: "he could not have said it better."

In response to a question about gender disparities, Young agreed that the issue needs to be addressed with families and with policy makers. Gender bias in a society can interact with child development programs in harmful ways—as when families pull their daughters from school because they believe that an early education program has taught their daughters all they need to know. Early childhood programs can send children along trajectories toward more equity, she said.

A questioner asked whether place-based programs can reach transient populations like the homeless or highly mobile children, and Young agreed that it is possible for such children to be left behind. She mentioned children in China left behind when their parents go to cities to work. In those cases, care providers need to work with governments to support these vulnerable population groups.

CREATING THE FUTURE OF EARLY
CHILDHOOD POLICY AND PRACTICE[3]

Jack P. Shonkoff
Harvard University

On the basis of a conceptual model developed by Julius Richmond, social change requires three things, said Jack P. Shonkoff, Director of the Center on the Developing Child at Harvard University. The first is a knowledge base, which *From Neurons to Neighborhoods* helped articulate 10 years ago and which has been growing ever since. The second is political will, which Shonkoff judged to be even stronger now than it was a decade ago, "notwithstanding all the constraints." The third is a social strategy, which constitutes the major challenge facing those who seek to chart the future of early childhood policy and practice.

---

[3] This section of the chapter is based on the presentation by Jack Shonkoff titled "Creating the Future of Early Childhood Policy and Practice" at *From Neurons to Neighborhoods* Anniversary: Ten Years Later.

Existing Social Strategies

Researchers, policy makers, and practitioners in the field of early childhood development currently employ a variety of social strategies, said Shonkoff. The question is how to design and implement new strategies that produce a higher magnitude of impact.

He discussed three strategies in particular. The first is to enhance the quality of the policies and programs that are in place and increase access to services. A tremendous amount of creative energy is directed toward this strategy. For example, the field no longer hesitates to address variability in the quality of programs, whereas when the political will was not as strong, it was dangerous to talk about poor-quality programs. "Now it is dangerous not to talk about the variability in quality," he observed.

The second strategy is to expand effective models. Taking good programs to scale requires creative thinking and effort. "This is a real challenge," Shonkoff said. "We need better strategies to take things to scale."

The third strategy, on which Shonkoff focused, is to build, test, and promote enhanced theories of change. This strategy was implicit in the original work on *From Neurons to Neighborhoods*, and it can be more explicit today, given that the science base is an even greater potential source of innovative ideas.

One benefit of this strategy is that it offers a way to examine and improve current approaches in early childhood intervention. For example, the most common current approach was established with the Great Society programs and has largely stood the test of time. It provides enriched opportunities for learning to children who may have limited access to such opportunities. It is also a two-generational approach, in that it provides education to parents about child development and parenting support. "With very few exceptions, everything that we do is a variation on that theme, and it continues to stand on a very solid scientific foundation," Shonkoff said.

A strategy of developing and testing new theories of change asks how the current approach can be strengthened. For example, research on the biology of adversity suggests a compelling new theory to enhance both learning and health (see Figure 3-2). Excessive activation of the body's stress response systems can lead to long-term disruptions in brain architecture, immune status, metabolic regulation, and cardiovascular function. Decreasing the number and severity of adverse early experiences and strengthening the relationships that protect young children from the harmful effects of toxic stress would therefore be expected to build stronger foundations for both learning and health.

"Developing and testing new approaches does not mean that enriched learning experiences are unimportant," Shonkoff said. "They are tremen-

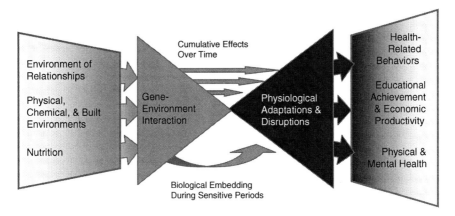

FIGURE 3-2 A biodevelopmental framework can relate the multiple influences during development to lifelong outcomes.
SOURCE: Center on the Developing Child at Harvard University, 2010b. Reprinted with permission. Copyright 2010 Center on the Developing Child at Harvard University.

dously important. But new thinking is needed to build on the best of current efforts and design new interventions that achieve greater impacts."

In pursuing innovative strategies, the business community can also be seen as a potential partner, rather than an antagonist, Shonkoff observed. In business, the most successful organizations know they are not going to stay at the top of their fields if they do not figure out how to be the first ones to do the next new thing. Actively pursuing innovation is not a sign of weakness but of strength.

A Partnership for Innovation

One way to translate a science base into more effective programs is to bring together people with diverse expertise. For example, the Center on the Developing Child, which Shonkoff directs, has been developing a joint initiative with the National Conference of State Legislatures and the National Governors Association Center for Best Practices. Those partners in turn brought in the TruePoint Center for High Performance and High Commitment to provide expertise in organizational system change, innovation, and the processes needed to move an innovation agenda. The result has been the Early Childhood Innovation Partnership, which is leveraging the science base to develop an innovation agenda that goes beyond current practices and policies.

The partnership has spent considerable time establishing priorities and has focused on three domains designed to reduce adversity and not just provide enrichment. The first is to reduce developmental barriers to learning. These are aspects of social and emotional development and executive functioning that interfere with children's ability to achieve full benefit from enriched learning opportunities. "We cannot simply provide enrichment; we also have to reduce barriers to healthy development," said Shonkoff.

The second focus area is to transform the lives of parents as a way of changing the lives of their children. Violence, mental health problems, substance abuse, and other factors are placing tremendous burdens on the lives of young children, particularly for the most vulnerable. Changing the life prospects of highly disadvantaged children requires more than parenting education, because simply providing information does not automatically change the circumstances of people who are dealing with significant stress-inducing circumstances.

The third area of focus is to reconceptualize the health dimension of early childhood policy and practice. Current policy for early childhood development remains centered on education—it is designed to prepare children to be ready to succeed in school. Current policy also has a health dimension, but it is largely focused on ensuring access to a regular source of medical care. Are the child's immunizations up to date? Have vision and hearing been screened? Has a child been examined for developmental problems or health impairments?

Speaking as a pediatrician, Shonkoff observed that education-centered interventions are obviously important, but early childhood does not just lay the foundation for learning. It also has long-term health consequences and can be a time in which the origins of lifelong health problems are established, including the precursors of cardiovascular disease, diabetes, hypertension, stroke, and other common chronic diseases. "The health dimension of early childhood is not just about medical care. It is about addressing the early roots of lifelong health and disease," he noted.

An Ecology of Innovation

One way to organize thinking about innovation in the field of early childhood development is through analogy with an ecological system, Shonkoff observed. At the first level, innovations occur in a particular "climate." For early childhood development, the climate for innovation is determined by public discourse in the policy arena and, more broadly, by public understanding of the field. It is important for people in positions of power, said Shonkoff, to understand why the early childhood period is so important and to establish priorities for the allocation of resources.

In that respect, today's climate is promising. "The policy climate for early childhood right now is very different from what it was 10 years ago. People get it—in a general sense—that early experience affects the developing architecture of the brain." However, the climate could be improved, Shonkoff pointed out. If policy makers understood the impact of behavior, emotion, and executive functioning on learning, there would no longer be a policy debate about whether early childhood programs should focus on cognitive skills *or* social and emotional development. Similarly, policy makers need to understand that the early childhood policy agenda is as much about health as it is about education. Such an understanding would make it possible to consider early childhood investments as relevant for both health and education budgets.

The second dimension of an ecology of innovation is "seeds." These are the breakthrough ideas currently being cultivated in "hot house" laboratories, whether those laboratories are in the university or in the community, that go beyond interventions currently being done, tested, or taken to scale. For example, the idea of improving child outcomes by transforming the economic and psychological capacities of their parents is one such seed. A lot of work has already been done in this area—particularly in services focused primarily on low-income women—but this work is not yet ready for replication in early childhood programs. "These intervention strategies are not yet ready to be tested in a randomized controlled trial," said Shonkoff. "We need further incubation of creative, new ideas before we conduct these kinds of trials."

Another innovation seed in the domain of health is the use of biomarkers to assess relative resilience and vulnerability, individualize services, and measure the effects of interventions. Such biomarkers include stress hormones, inflammatory proteins, cardiovascular reactivity, epigenetic markers, and neuroimaging, among others. Much work still needs to be done to develop these biomarkers before they can be used in community-based settings, as the use of measures without knowing their full meaning raises ethical as well as scientific questions. But research on biomarkers is generating considerable interest and excitement. For example, could biomarkers measure the impacts of toxic stress on young children or differentiate those who are in trouble from those who are not? This work is definitely not ready for programmatic application, but it certainly is important to pursue in a responsible manner, Shonkoff said.

The third aspect of an ecology is "soil"—the people and places who constitute a receptive environment to try a new idea. "If we are using science to incubate seeds, then we need places that provide rich soil where you can plant some of these seeds and evaluate whether they grow." If the soil is not receptive, the failure of a program may be blamed on the program itself and not on the conditions under which it was implemented. Communities and states that want to try new things provide promising soil for innovation. "We can't try new things everywhere, and we can't try new things in places that don't want to take risks, so we have to utilize those settings that want to be the pioneers."

The Benefits of Programmatic Focus

The priorities selected by the Early Childhood Innovation Partnership are a subset of the many new ideas worth trying that could have concrete benefits for multiple constituencies. Shonkoff identified four potential benefits of pursuing these priorities.

First, policy makers want evidence of interventions that produce impacts on school readiness and on educational achievement. They are looking for new ways to promote health and prevent disease, not just pay for expensive care for people who are sick.

Second, the people who work in early childhood programs on a day-to-day basis are eager for new things to try. Many are trying new interventions themselves, but they have few ways of disseminating ideas that work well. Also, some people may try new things, but the ability of science to explain why these things work can be the crucial impetus to change. "If people are trying things that seem to have significant impacts, it would be great for scientists to be in there to figure out the explanation as to why they are working," Shonkoff said.

Third, trying out new ideas will make it possible to leverage the science of early childhood development across a wide range of sectors and outcomes. "It is not just about learning, it is not just about behavior, it is not just about health. We can deal with all these domains simultaneously," he noted.

Finally, and more speculatively, if researchers can figure out how to use technology to measure the biological impacts of an intervention, they could transform the evaluation of alternative approaches to promoting early childhood development. For example, science would "not have to wait for a 50-year follow-up study to show that we have the capacity to reduce the risk of heart disease," Shonkoff observed. "That would be a tremendous new contribution to the field."

Discussion

Shonkoff was asked what the United States can learn from other countries in establishing programs and policies that affect early childhood development, and he pointed out that many countries have established promising early childhood initiatives that are worthy of examination. However, the United States has a more individualistic political culture than do many other countries and therefore does not necessarily look abroad for policy guidance. "That is just the reality," he said, "without passing a judgment on it one way or the other." The challenge is to develop a strategy that reflects the political culture of the United States.

It is also important to remember that in early childhood development, much of the action in the United States occurs at the state rather than federal level. Federal policy and funding certainly have tremendous influence, but most important decisions are made by state officials, and it can be more manageable to work with leaders at that level. In addition, by working at the state level, new ideas can be instituted in places that are more hospitable to them. For example, the Early Childhood Innovation Partnership is currently working with a state to connect its child welfare system to a larger health agenda, in part using funds and guidelines provided through the new federal health care law. Shonkoff stated, "This is simply a matter of building relationships with people who want to try new things—and then rolling up our sleeves and getting to work. We don't have illusions about sending people scientific papers and expecting things to change. . . . Our strategy is to find places that want to exhibit leadership through innovation, explore what is possible, and then use successful achievements as examples for other places."

A logic model for the development of effective policy needs to emphasize both people and programs. Governments do not make children healthier. It is what the government does to strengthen the capacity of caregivers in a child's life or a community in which a child lives that has an effect on health. This emphasizes causal mechanisms while also providing an opportunity for more politically persuasive, broadly based, and bipartisan arguments.

Shonkoff also commented on the potential for conflicts among the needs of young children and adolescents across different age groups. He said it is a mistake to talk about any one period as being more important than any other period. Brain development proceeds continually throughout the early years of life, into adolescence, and through adulthood. Thus, investing only in a single period can result in gains lost when that period is over. At the moment, early childhood receives fewer societal investments than do other periods of life, which makes it harder to build a strong foundation for later development. But that does not mean that one period is more important than another. *From Neurons to Neighborhoods*, in focusing on the first few years of life, made this point by saying that from a developmental perspective, a policy focus on the period from birth to age 3 is starting too late and ending too early.

Focusing on a single age period also can send the mistaken message that irreversible damage can be done if interventions are lacking at that age. There is plasticity in the brain throughout life, so children should not be stigmatized by saying that an irreplaceable opportunity has been missed.

4

Final Remarks

From Neurons to Neighborhoods was grounded in four overarching themes:

1. All children are born wired for feelings and ready to learn.
2. Early environments matter and nurturing relationships are essential.
3. Society is changing and the needs of young children are not being addressed.
4. Interactions among early childhood science, policy, and practice are problematic and demand dramatic rethinking.

The first two themes have held up well over the past decade, said Jack Shonkoff in his concluding remarks at the workshop. Researchers have learned much more about development of the brain in early childhood, and this understanding will continue to expand in the future. They also have achieved a much deeper and richer understanding of the importance of early environments and nurturing relationships. "Two of the four themes have stood the test of time," Shonkoff said.

The other two themes have become even more urgent in the years since *From Neurons to Neighborhoods* appeared. These were the two themes that put the scientific principles in a social context, and society has been changing even faster than it has in the past. Shonkoff cited one alarming example: the rise of child poverty over the past decade, with bleak prospects for significant improvement in the near future. Many people have lost their jobs in the recent recession and will not get them back for a long time. And high school graduation rates are still only about 50 percent in most inner cities, and a high school diploma alone is no longer a ticket to a good job in U.S. society.

Shonkoff said that he would now change the wording of the fourth theme slightly. Rather than saying that interactions among early childhood science, policy, and practice are problematic, he would now say that they are complex. That is to say, these dynamics are somewhat less problematic than they were in the past because there is much more interaction among the three sectors. However, these increased interactions have demonstrated how complex both the problems and the potential solutions really are.

Science has informed policy and practice in invigorating and productive ways. But the flow of information has been largely one way, in that policy and practice have not much influenced the kinds of questions researchers are asking. The challenge for the scientific community is to respond to new ideas that are driving progress in the field. How exactly does experience affect health or learning? What are the features of effective interventions? The policy community will be much more willing to invest in early childhood interventions if it understands why a certain program produces a positive outcome.

The early childhood development community can be simultaneously proud and dissatisfied with how far it has come, Shonkoff said. Science, policy, and practice have all made great advances in the past 10 years. The remaining challenge is to continue to translate new knowledge into new ideas that will dramatically improve the lives of children and their prospects for the future.

References

Brown, D. W., R. F. Anda, H. Tiemeier, V. J. Felitti, V. J. Edwards, J. B. Croft, and W. H. Giles. 2009. Adverse childhood experiences and the risk of premature mortality. *American Journal of Preventive Medicine* 37(5):389-396.

Center on the Developing Child at Harvard University. 2010a. *The foundations of lifelong health are built in early childhood*. Cambridge, MA: Center on the Developing Child at Harvard University.

Center on the Developing Child at Harvard University. 2010b. *How early experiences get into the body: A biodevelopmental framework*. http://developingchild.harvard.edu/resources/multimedia/interactive_features/biodevelopmental-framework/ (accessed March 5, 2012).

Commission on Social Determinants of Health. 2008. *Closing the gap in a generation: Health equity through action on the social determinants of health. Final report of the Commission on Social Determinants of Health*. Geneva: World Health Organization.

Engle, P. L., M. M. Black, J. R. Behrman, M. Cabral de Mello, P. J. Gertler, L. Kapiriri, R. Martorell, and M. E. Young. 2007. Strategies to avoid the loss of developmental potential in more than 200 million children in the developing world. *The Lancet* 369(9557):229-242.

Grantham-McGregor, S., Y. B. Cheung, S. Cueto, P. Glewwe, L. Richter, and B. Strupp. 2007. Developmental potential in the first 5 years for children in developing countries. *The Lancet* 369(9555):60-70.

Jolly, R. 2007. Early childhood development: The global challenge. *The Lancet* 369(9555):8-9.

Lombardi, J. 2010 (October 28). *The impact and promise of early childhood science: A federal policy perspective*. Paper presented at *From Neurons to Neighborhoods* Anniversary: Ten Years Later, Washington, DC.

McEwen, B. S. 1998. Protective and damaging effects of stress mediators. *New England Journal of Medicine* 338(3):171-179.

McEwen, B. 2010 (October 28). *Stress and the central role of the brain*. Paper presented at *From Neurons to Neighborhoods* Anniversary: Ten Years Later, Washington, DC.

NRC (National Research Council). 2009. *Mathematics learning in early childhood: Paths toward excellence and equity*. Washington, DC: The National Academies Press.

NRC and IOM (Institute of Medicine). 2000. *From neurons to neighborhoods: The science of early childhood development.* Washington, DC: National Academy Press.

Shonkoff, J. P., W. T. Boyce, and B. S. McEwen. 2009. Neuroscience, molecular biology, and the childhood roots of health disparities. *Journal of the American Medical Association* 301(21):2252-2259.

Stipek, D. 2010 (October 28). *Learning.* Paper presented at *From Neurons to Neighborhoods* Anniversary: Ten Years Later, Washington, DC.

Walker, S. P., T. D. Wachs, J. Meeks Gardner, B. Lozoff, G. A. Wasserman, E. Pollitt, and J. A. Carter. 2007. Child development: Risk factors for adverse outcomes in developing countries. *The Lancet* 369(9556):145-157.

Appendix A

Original Committee
Membership and Charge

**COMMITTEE ON INTEGRATING THE SCIENCE
OF EARLY CHILDHOOD DEVELOPMENT**

Jack P. Shonkoff, M.D. (*Chair*), Julius B. Richmond FAMRI Professor
in Child Health and Development, Center on the Developing Child,
Harvard University

Greg J. Duncan, Ph.D., Distinguished Professor of Education, Department
of Education, University of California, Irvine

Felton J. (Tony) Earls, M.D., Professor of Human Behavior and
Development, Department of Society, Human Development and
Health, School of Public Health, Harvard University

Robert N. Emde, M.D., Professor of Psychiatry, Emeritus, School of
Public Health, University of Colorado

Yolanda Garcia, M.A., M.S., Director, E3 Institute Advancing Excellence
in Early Education, WestEd, San Jose, California

Susan Gelman, Ph.D., Frederick G.L. Huetwell Professor of Psychology,
Department of Psychology, University of Michigan

Susan J. Goldin-Meadow, Ph.D., Beardsley Ruml Distinguished Service
Professor, Department of Psychology, The University of Chicago

William T. Greenough, Ph.D., Swanlund Professor and Director, Center
for Advanced Study, Department of Psychology and Beckman
Institute, University of Illinois at Urbana-Champaign

Megan Gunnar, Ph.D., Professor of Child Development, Institute of Child
Development, University of Minnesota

Michael J. Guralnick, Ph.D., Director, Center on Human Development
   and Disability, University of Washington
Alicia F. Lieberman, Ph.D., Irving B. Harris Endowed Chair in Infant
   Mental Health, Department of Psychiatry, University of California,
   San Francisco
Betsy Lozoff, M.D., Professor of Pediatrics, Center for Human Growth
   and Development, University of Michigan
Ruth W. Massinga, M.S., Former President and CEO, Casey Family
   Programs, Seattle
Stephen W. Raudenbush, Ed.D., Lewis-Sebring Distinguished Service
   Professor, Department of Sociology, The University of Chicago
Ross Allen Thompson, Ph.D., Professor, Department of Psychology,
   University of California, Davis
Deborah L. Vietz, Ph.D., Professor of Psychology, Department of
   Psychology, The Graduate Center, The City University of New York

COMMITTEE CHARGE

The Committee on Integrating the Science of Early Childhood Development was established by the Board on Children, Youth, and Families of the Institute of Medicine and the National Research Council to update scientific knowledge about the nature of early development and the role of early experiences, to disentangle such knowledge from erroneous popular beliefs or misunderstandings, and to discuss the implications of this knowledge base for early childhood policy, practice, professional development, and research.

Appendix B

Workshop Agenda and Participants

From Neurons to Neighborhoods Anniversary:
Ten Years Later

Thursday, October 28, 2010

Welcome and Introductions

Panel 1   What We've Learned: The Impact and Promise of Early
          Childhood Science
          *Moderator: Deborah A. Phillips, Ph.D., Professor of
          Psychology, Georgetown University*

          The Federal Policy Perspective
              Joan Lombardi, Ph.D., Deputy Assistant Secretary for Early
              Childhood Development, U.S. Department of Health and
              Human Services

              Alan E. Guttmacher, M.D., Director, Eunice Kennedy
              Shriver National Institute of Child Health and Human
              Development

Implications for Physical and Mental Health
Bruce S. McEwen, Ph.D., Alfred E. Mirsky Professor,
Rockefeller University

Implications for Motivation and Learning
Deborah J. Stipek, Ph.D., James Quillen Dean and Professor
of Education, Stanford University

General Discussion with Audience

Panel 2   Where Do We Go from Here: Mobilizing Science to Promote
Innovation
*Moderator: Bernard Guyer, M.D., Zanvyl Kreiger Professor of
Children's Health, Johns Hopkins University, and Chair, IOM-
NRC Board on Children, Youth, and Families*

Lessons Learned from a Global Perspective
Mary Eming Young, M.D., Dr.P.H., Lead Child
Development Specialist, The World Bank's Human
Development Network

Creating the Future of Early Childhood Policy and Practice
Jack P. Shonkoff, M.D., Director, Center on the Developing
Child, Harvard University

General Discussion with Audience

Closing Remarks
Jack P. Shonkoff, M.D.

PARTICIPANTS

Planning Committee

Jack P. Shonkoff (*Chair*), Center on the Developing Child, Harvard
University
Huda Akil, The Molecular and Behavioral Neuroscience Institute,
University of Michigan
Debbie Chang, Nemours Health and Prevention Services
Bernard Guyer, Bloomberg School of Public Health, Johns Hopkins
University
Ruth Massinga, Casey Family Programs

Bruce McEwen, Harold and Margaret Milliken Hatch Laboratory of Neuroendocrinology, Rockefeller University
Pamela Morris, Department of Applied Psychology, New York University
Deborah Phillips, Department of Psychology, Georgetown University

National Academies Staff

Rosemary Chalk, Director, Board on Children, Youth, and Families
Pamella Atayi, Senior Program Assistant
Reine Homawoo, Senior Program Assistant
Wendy Keenan, Program Associate
Rachel Pittluck, Senior Program Assistant

Invited Participants

Larry Adelman, California Newsreel
Nancy Adler, University of California, San Francisco
Aida Balsano, National Institute of Food and Agriculture
Cecilia Barbosa, Virginia Commonwealth University
Shari Barkin, Vanderbilt University
Moushumi Beltangady, Administration for Children and Families, U.S. Department of Health and Human Services
Dara Blachman, Centers for Disease Control and Prevention
Rosemary Bolig, University of the District of Columbia
Caliste Boswell, Voices for America's Children
Marion Burton, American Academy of Pediatrics
Mia Smith Bynum, University of Maryland
Karen Cadigan, University of Minnesota
Mary Campbell, American Psychological Association
Jeffrey Capizzano, Administration for Children and Families, U.S. Department of Health and Human Services
Beth Caron, U.S. Department of Education
Ann Carroll, U.S. Environmental Protection Agency
BJ Casey, Weill Medical College of Cornell University
Jasmine Chan, Student
Katy Chapman, U.S. Department of Education
Alice Luo Clayton, National Institute of Mental Health
Steffanie Clothier, National Conference of State Legislatures
Anne DeBiasi, Nemours Foundation
Rachel Demma, National Governors Association
Harriet Dichter, First Five Years Fund
Libby Doggett, Pew Center on the States
Denise Dougherty, Agency for Healthcare Research and Quality

Alison Earle, Northeastern University
Julia Martin Eile, U.S. Department of Education
Robert N. Emde, University of Colorado
Valerie Estep, Voices for America's Children
Gary Evans, Cornell University
Stephanie Fanjul, National Association for the Education of Young
     Children/North Carolina Partnership for Children
Lauren Fasig, University of Florida
Christine Ferguson, George Washington University
Amy Fine, Consultant
Nathaniel Foote, TruePoint
Lisa Freund, Eunice Kennedy Shriver National Institute of Child Health
     and Human Development, National Institutes of Health
Sarah Friedman, CNA Corporation
Yolanda Garcia, WestEd
Melody Gilbert, Association of Maternal and Child Health Programs
Tia Gilbert, Administration for Children and Families, U.S. Department
     of Health and Human Services
Sherry Glied, Office of the Assistant Secretary for Planning and
     Evaluation, U.S. Department of Health and Human Services
Phyllis Glink, The Harris Foundation
Stacie Goffin, Goffin Strategy Group
Alice Ann Gola, Georgetown University
Naomi Goldstein, Administration for Children and Families,
     U.S. Department of Health and Human Services
Rosie Gomez, Children's Bureau, U.S. Department of Health and Human
     Services
Richard Gonzales, Administration for Children and Families,
     U.S. Department of Health and Human Services
Cathy Grace, Children's Defense Fund
Jim Griffin, Eunice Kennedy Shriver National Institute of Child Health
     and Human Development, National Institutes of Health
Eugenia Grohman, National Research Council
Deborah Gross, Johns Hopkins University
Megan Gunnar, University of Minnesota
Alan Guttmacher, Eunice Kennedy Shriver National Institute of Child
     Health and Human Development, National Institutes of Health
Meredith Hanley, Committee for Economic Development
Jodi Hardin, Colorado Department of Public Health and Environment
Samantha Harvell, First Focus
Robert M. Hauser, National Research Council and University of
     Wisconsin
Laura Helmuth, Smithsonian Magazine

David Heppel, Health Resources and Services Administration,
    U.S. Department of Health and Human Services
Steven Hicks, U.S. Department of Education
Gail R. Houle, U.S. Department of Education
Mengfei Huang, National Institutes of Health
Dannie James, JE Group/GBC
Sarah Joestl, National Institute of Mental Health
Jacqueline Jones, U.S. Department of Education
Christy Kavulic, Office of Special Education Programs
Linda Kilroy, National Academies
Lisa G. Klein, Birth to Five Policy Alliance
Nancy Landale, Pennsylvania State University
Nicole Lander, Voices for America's Children
Suzanne Landi, Institute of Medicine
Judy Langford, Center for the Study of Social Policy
Sara Langworthy, University of Minnesota
Michele Lawler, Health Resources and Services Administration,
    U.S. Department of Health and Human Services
Cindy Lederman, Eleventh Judicial Circuit Court of Florida
Melinda Leidy, Administration for Children and Families,
    U.S. Department of Health and Human Services
Joan Lombardi, Administration for Children and Families,
    U.S. Department of Health and Human Services
Betsy Lozoff, University of Michigan
Sarah Lynne-Landsman, National Institute on Drug Abuse
Coretta Mallery, American Institutes for Research
Nancy Mannix, Norlien Foundation
Ronald N. Mannix, Norlien Foundation
Nancy Margie, Administration for Children and Families,
    U.S. Department of Health and Human Services
Jana Martella, National Association of Early Childhood Specialists in
    State Departments of Education
Ann S. Masten, University of Minnesota
Mary Ann McCabe, George Washington University
Stephanie McGencey, Grantmakers for Children, Youth, and Families
J. Michael McGinnis, Institute of Medicine
Kim Means, Office of Head Start, U.S. Department of Health and Human
    Services
Lorrie Meier, Consultant
Matthew Melmed, Zero To Three
Diana Morales, National Institute of Mental Health
Taryn Morrissey, American University
Mojdeh Motamedi, American Institutes for Research

Velma McBride Murry, Vanderbilt University
Gillian Najarian, Harvard University
Bergen Nelson, Administration for Children and Families,
     U.S. Department of Health and Human Services
Wendy Nilsen, Office of Behavioral and Social Sciences Research,
     National Institutes of Health
Catherine Nolan, Administration for Children and Families,
     U.S. Department of Health and Human Services
Jean Nussbaum, Administration for Children and Families,
     U.S. Department of Health and Human Services
Michael Oberdorfer, Consultant
Devin O'Connor, U.S. Department of Health and Human Services
Nina Sazer O'Donnell, United Way Worldwide
Steve Olson, Rapporteur
Leslie Oppenheimer, Center for Young Children Laboratory School
Shiek Pal, Office of the State Superintendent of Education
Diana Pankevich, Institute of Medicine
Robin Parsell, Institute of Medicine
Deepali Patel, Institute of Medicine
Daniel Pedersen, Buffett Early Childhood Fund
Ruth Perou, Centers for Disease Control and Prevention
Marge Petruska, The Heinz Endowments
Jessica Ramakis, U.S. Department of Education
Gail Ritchie, Substance Abuse and Mental Health Services
     Administration, U.S. Department of Health and Human Services
Adele Robinson, National Association for the Education of Young
     Children
Christine Robinson, Stillwaters Consultation
Miriam Rollin, Fight Crime: Invest in Kids
Ann Rosewater, Consultant
Lisa Rubenstein, Substance Abuse and Mental Health Services
     Administration, U.S. Department of Health and Human Services
Stephanie Schaefer, Fight Crime: Invest in Kids
Edward Schor, The Commonwealth Fund
Lee Schorr, Center for the Study of Social Policy
Karen Schulman, National Women's Law Center
Tom Schultz, Council of Chief State School Officers
Lonnie Sherrod, Society for Research on Child Development
Eva Marie Shivers, Indigo Cultural Center
Howard Silver, Consortium of Social Science Associations
Cara Sklar, Office of the State Superintendent of Education
Dori Sneddon, Administration for Children and Families,
     U.S. Department of Health and Human Services

Douglas Sprunger, National Research Council
Kam Sripada, Administration for Children and Families,
    U.S. Department of Health and Human Services
Helene Stebbins, Birth to Five Policy Alliance
Elaine Stedt, Administration for Children and Families,
    U.S. Department of Health and Human Services
Kate Stepleton, Administration for Children and Families,
    U.S. Department of Health and Human Services
Michelle Sternthal, U.S. Department of Housing and Urban Development
Deborah Stipek, Stanford University
Susanne Stoiber, Stoiber Health Policy, LLC
Jonah Stuart, Teaching Strategies, Inc.
Maurice Sykes, University of the District of Columbia
Amanda Szekely, National Governors Association
Louisa Tarullo, Mathematica Policy Research
Alicia Thomas, Grantmakers in Health
Lauren Tobias, Institute of Medicine
Jennifer Tschantz, U.S. Department of Education
Douglas Tynan, Nemours Health and Prevention Services
Jon Vaupel, U.S. Department of Education
Ellen Wartella, Northwestern University
Sara Watson, Pew Charitable Trusts
Mary Bruce Webb, Administration for Children and Families,
    U.S. Department of Health and Human Services
Tisha Wiley, Office of Behavioral and Social Sciences Research,
    National Institutes of Health
Judy Willgren, U.S. Department of Health and Human Services
David Willis, American Academy of Pediatrics
Hirokazu Yoshikawa, Harvard University
Marci Young, Pre-K Now
Mary Eming Young, The World Bank
Francie Zimmerman, Doris Duke Charitable Foundation